french

french

THE TRUE TASTE OF FRANCE IN CLASSIC REGIONAL DISHES

foreword by
marie-pierre moine

LORENZ BOOKS

Published by Lorenz Books
an imprint of Anness Publishing Limited
Hermes House, 88-89 Blackfriars Road, London SE1 8HA

This edition distributed in Canada by Raincoast Books
8680 Cambie Street, Vancouver, British Columbia V6P 6M9

ISBN 0-7548-0043-1

Publisher Joanna Lorenz
Senior Cookery Editor Linda Fraser
Cookery Editor Anne Hildyard
Designer Nigel Partridge
Illustrations Madeleine David
Photographers Karl Adamson, Edward Allwright, Steve Baxter, Amanda Heywood and Michael Michaels
Recipes Carla Capalbo, Roz Denny, Christine France, Sarah Gates, Shirley Gill, Norma MacMillan, Laura Washburn and Steven Wheeler
Food for photography Elizabeth Wolf-Cohen, Wendy Lee and Jane Stevenson
Stylists Hilary Guy, Blake Minton and Kirsty Rawlings
Cover: *Photography* Nicki Dowey *Food Stylist* Emma Patmore *Design* Wilson Harvey

Typeset by MC Typeset Ltd, Rochester, Kent
Printed and bound in Singapore

Also published as part of the *Classic* series

1 3 5 7 9 10 8 6 4 2

For all recipes, quantities are given in both metric and imperial measures, and, where appropriate, measures are also given in standard cups and spoons. Follow one set, but not a mixture, because they are not interchangeable.

Pictures on frontispiece, pages 8 and 9: Zefa Pictures Ltd.
Picture on page 7: Michael Busselle

Contents

Foreword

There is something about the home cooking of France which always conjures up the flavours, smells and sounds of my childhood. When I started reading this cookbook, the recipes and their introductions brought back happy memories. That first encounter with pine nuts in the scented hot shrublands behind the Mediterranean coast, an early morning bicycle ride through lush Normandy pastures and a Camembert tasting at Pont-Audemer market, an autumn afternoon train journey followed by a meal that concluded with the best chocolate profiteroles I ever ate – the selection of recipes successfully evoked recollections of the French countryside.

When I looked at the recipes more critically, as an expatriate cook, I also appreciated the fact that despite being genuinely French, they were also accessible for kitchens anywhere in the world. Here is a collection of dishes you can very easily re-create at home with supermarket ingredients. Some recipes have been given a little twist to make them exciting for more adventurous modern tastebuds: crispy potato cakes are paired with goat's cheese, curried mussels are delectably combined with lentils, sole goujons are enhanced by a sharp lime mayonnaise. Old favourites, those authentic dishes that cannot really be improved on, are presented in traditional but feasible versions. Try such dishes as Trout with Mushroom Sauce, Onion Tart, Breton Pork and Bean Casserole or Apricot and Almond Jalousie, and discover the essence of French home cooking at its best.

Marie-Pierre Moine

ORTS
RÉSERVÉ
AU SERVICE
PUBLIC

INTRODUCTION

France is deservedly famous for its excellent food, and travelling through France, sampling regional dishes, is a true treat for the tastebuds.

The very size of the country means there are considerable variations in terms of climate and landscape. Ever since the time when poor communications made every region dependent on its own produce, each area has had its own specialities. Markets are a marvellous source of basic raw ingredients, which are always chosen with considerable care, be they fresh vegetables, fruit, wines or cheeses. France is renowned for its cheeses. Every region has its own, made from cow's, goat's or ewe's milk and varying from soft and creamy to hard and strong.

The Brittany coastline is well known for its abundant seafood, particularly shellfish such as mussels, crabs, lobsters and oysters. Seafood, especially sole, also comes from neighbouring Normandy, a region equally notable for its rich dairy pastures. Famous cheeses like Camembert, Pont-L'Evêque and Neufchâtel are produced here, along with rich butter, crème fraîche (the thick, slightly acidic cream) and fresh cream cheeses such as fromage blanc. Normandy is also famous for its apple orchards, the fruit of which is made into cider and Calvados. Benedictine, the herb liqueur, is another Norman speciality. The meat of the region is excellent, especially pork and lamb. The popular tripe dish, *Tripes à la Mode de Caen,* is famous the world over.

Apart from the obvious, Champagne is known for charcuterie, including smoked and stuffed tongue, and game, while Lorraine lends its name to a number of dishes, including the famous quiche. Alsace numbers pork, goose, game and choucroute (pickled cabbage) among its specialities, whereas the Burgundy region

Well ripened garlic and lemons for sale on a market stall (left), vines planted in neat rows, stretch as far as the eye can see (above), and an interesting selection of French cheeses in a typical Paris market (right).

produces not only fine wines, but also beef and chickens, hence the recipe for Coq au Vin in this book. This is also the home of snails and Dijon mustard. From the Auvergne comes a large variety of cheeses, and also potatoes, cabbages, lentils, ham, sausages and pork products. The cows of the mountainous Savoie produce more milk than the population can drink, so this area is known for its gratin dishes using milk, cream and cheese. Comté cheese, walnuts, chestnuts, fruit, dried beef and wild mushrooms also come from here.

Further south is Provence, an area world-renowned for its colourful, piquant dishes. Olives and olive oil, tomatoes, onions, garlic and herbs are ingredients that find their way into a range of recipes, including Salade Niçoise and Mediterranean Fish Stew.

The south west is one of the great larders of France, producing lamb, Bayonne ham, beef, duck, chicken, onions, prunes, peaches, pears, grapes and seafood, especially squid, sardines, anchovies and oysters.

Bordeaux is known for its fine wines and Cognac, while not far away, in the Dordogne, the specialities are geese, ducks and truffles (often used in pâtés), nuts and fruit. In the Loire valley, both vegetables and fruits are grown, and from its river come freshwater fish such as trout. This is also the region where the legendary Tarte Tatin, with its delicious topping of caramelized apples, was first created.

From the Loire it is but a short step to Brittany, where our whistle-stop culinary tour began. As the recipes amply illustrate, France is indeed a country where one is spoilt for choice.

Leek Terrine with Deli Meats

Terrine de Poireaux Charcutière

This attractive starter is very simple to make yet looks spectacular. You can make the terrine a day ahead and keep it covered in the fridge. If your guests are vegetarian offer a selection of French cheeses instead of sliced meats.

Ingredients

20–24 small young leeks
60ml/4 tbsp walnut oil
60ml/4 tbsp olive oil
30ml/2 tbsp white wine vinegar
5ml/1 tsp wholegrain mustard
about 225g/8oz sliced meats, such as Jambon de Bayonne *or* Jambon de Toulouse
50g/2oz/⅔ cup walnuts, toasted and chopped
salt and ground black pepper

Serves 6

Cook's tip

For this terrine, it is important to use tender young leeks. The white part mainly is used in this recipe, but the green tops can be used in soups. The terrine must be pressed for at least 4 hours – to make it easier to slice.

1 Cut off the roots and most of the green part from the leeks. Wash thoroughly under cold running water. Bring a large pan of salted water to the boil. Add the leeks, bring the water back to the boil, then reduce the heat and simmer for 6–8 minutes, until the leeks are just tender. Drain well.

2 Fill a 450g/1lb loaf tin with the leeks, placing them alternately head to tail, to create a patterned effect, and sprinkling each layer with salt and pepper as you go.

3 Put another loaf tin inside the first one and gently press down on the leeks. Carefully invert both tins and let any water drain out. Place one or two kitchen weights or heavy cans on top of the tins and chill the terrine for at least 4 hours, or overnight.

4 Meanwhile, to make the dressing, spoon the walnut and olive oils, wine vinegar and wholegrain mustard into a small bowl, add salt and pepper, and whisk together. Taste for seasoning and add more salt and pepper if required.

5 Carefully turn out the terrine on to a board and cut into slices using a large sharp knife. Lay the slices of leek terrine on serving plates and arrange the slices of meat alongside. Spoon the dressing over the slices of terrine and scatter over the chopped walnuts. Serve immediately.

Onion Soup

Soupe à l'Oignon

Recipes for onion soup vary around the world, but this is the absolute classic – once the morning pick-me-up for workers at Les Halles, the food market in central Paris.

Ingredients

30ml/2 tbsp butter
15ml/1 tbsp oil
3 large onions, thinly sliced
5ml/1 tsp soft brown sugar
15ml/1 tbsp flour
2 × 275g/10oz cans condensed beef consommé
30ml/2 tbsp medium sherry
10ml/2 tsp Worcestershire sauce
8 slices French bread
15ml/1 tbsp wholegrain mustard
115g/4oz/1 cup Gruyère cheese, grated
salt and ground black pepper
chopped fresh parsley, to garnish

Serves 4

1 Heat the butter and oil in a large pan and add the onions and brown sugar. Cook gently for about 20 minutes, stirring occasionally, until the onions start to turn golden brown.

2 Stir in the flour and cook for a further 2 minutes. Pour in the consommé, plus two cans of water, then add the sherry and Worcestershire sauce. Season well, cover, and simmer gently for 25–30 minutes.

Variation

Omit the mustard and, instead, rub the croûtes on each side with the cut side of a garlic clove before adding the Gruyère cheese.

3 Preheat the grill and, just before serving, toast the bread lightly on both sides. Spread one side of each slice with the mustard and top with the grated cheese. Grill the toasts until bubbling and golden.

4 Ladle the soup into soup plates. Place two croûtes on top of each plate of soup and garnish with chopped fresh parsley. Serve at once.

CAMEMBERT FRITTERS

Beignets de Camembert

These deep-fried cheeses are simple to prepare. They are served with a red onion marmalade which can be made in advance and stored in the fridge.

INGREDIENTS

8 individual portions of Camembert
1 egg, beaten
115g/4oz/1 cup dried breadcrumbs, to coat
oil, for deep-frying
parsley sprigs, to garnish

FOR THE MARMALADE

45ml/3 tbsp sunflower oil
45ml/3 tbsp olive oil
900g/2lb red onions, sliced
15ml/1 tbsp coriander seeds, crushed
2 bay leaves
45ml/3 tbsp granulated sugar
90ml/6 tbsp red wine vinegar
10ml/2 tsp salt

SERVES 4

1 To make the marmalade, heat the oils in a large saucepan and gently fry the onions, covered, for 20 minutes or until soft. Add the remaining ingredients, stir well, and cook, uncovered, for 10–15 minutes until most of the liquid is absorbed. Leave to cool.

2 To prepare the cheese, scratch the rinds lightly with a fork. Dip first in egg and then in breadcrumbs to coat well. Dip and coat a second time if necessary. Set aside.

3 Pour oil into a deep-fat fryer to one-third full and heat to 190°C/375°F. Add the cheeses a few at a time and fry for about 2 minutes until golden. Drain on kitchen paper and fry the rest of the cheeses, reheating the oil in between. Serve hot with the marmalade. Garnish with parsley sprigs.

COOK'S TIP

You could make these fritters with fingers of firm Brie, or try using small rounds of goat's cheese.

Spinach Salad with Bacon and Prawns

Salade d'Epinards à la Poitrine Fumée et aux Crevettes

Serve this warm salad with plenty of crusty bread for mopping up the delicious juices. It tastes every bit as good as it looks.

INGREDIENTS

105ml/7 tbsp olive oil
30ml/2 tbsp sherry vinegar
2 garlic cloves, finely chopped
5ml/1 tsp Dijon mustard
12 cooked unshelled king prawns
115g/4oz streaky bacon, rinded and cut into strips
about 115g/4oz fresh young spinach leaves
½ head oak-leaf lettuce, roughly torn
salt and ground black pepper

SERVES 4

1 To make the dressing, whisk together 90ml/6 tbsp of the olive oil with the vinegar, garlic, mustard and seasoning in a small pan. Heat gently until thickened slightly, then keep warm.

2 Carefully pull off the heads, then remove the shells and legs from the prawns, leaving the tails intact. Set aside.

3 Heat the remaining oil in a frying pan and fry the bacon until golden and crisp, stirring occasionally. Add the prawns and stir-fry for a few minutes until warmed through.

4 Meanwhile, arrange the spinach and torn oak-leaf lettuce leaves on four individual serving plates.

5 Spoon the bacon and prawns on to the salad leaves, then pour over the hot dressing. Serve at once.

RED ONION GALETTES

Galettes à l'Oignon Rouge

To give these savoury pastries a sharp edge, scatter some chopped anchovies over them before baking.

INGREDIENTS

60–75ml/4–5 tbsp olive oil
500g/1¼ lb red onions, sliced
1 garlic clove, crushed
30ml/2 tbsp chopped fresh mixed herbs, such as thyme, parsley and basil
225g/8oz ready-made puff pastry
15ml/1 tbsp sun-dried tomato paste
ground black pepper
thyme sprigs, to garnish

SERVES 4

1 Heat 30ml/2 tbsp of the oil in a pan and add the onions and garlic. Cook, covered, for 15–20 minutes, stirring occasionally, until soft but not browned. Stir in the herbs.

2 Preheat the oven to 220°C/425°F/Gas 7. Divide the pastry into four equal pieces and roll out each one to a 15cm/6in round on a lightly floured surface.

3 Flute the edges by crimping them with your fingers *(left)*. Prick all over with a fork. Place the rounds on baking sheets and chill them for 10 minutes.

4 Mix 15ml/1 tbsp of the remaining olive oil with the sun-dried tomato paste and brush over the centres of the rounds, leaving a 1cm/½in border. Spread the onion mixture over the pastry rounds and grind over plenty of pepper. Drizzle over a little more oil, then bake for about 15 minutes, until the pastry is crisp and golden. Serve hot, garnished with thyme sprigs.

Potato Cakes with Goat's Cheese

Petites Galettes de Pommes de Terre au Chèvre

Crispy potato cakes form the base of this melt-in-your-mouth starter. The goat's cheese and green salad transform it from the peasant dish it was originally to *haute cuisine.*

INGREDIENTS

450g/1lb potatoes, coarsely grated
10ml/2 tsp chopped fresh thyme
1 garlic clove, crushed
2 spring onions, finely chopped
30ml/2 tbsp olive oil
50g/2oz/4 tbsp unsalted butter
2 × 65g/2½oz Crottins de Chavignol (firm goat's cheeses)
salt and ground black pepper
thyme sprigs, to garnish
mixed green salad, to serve

SERVES 2–4

1 Using your hands, squeeze out the moisture from the potatoes, then carefully combine with the chopped thyme, garlic, spring onions and seasoning.

2 Heat half the oil and butter in a non-stick frying pan. Add two large spoonfuls of the potato mixture and press firmly down with a spoon. Cook for 3–4 minutes on each side until golden.

3 Drain the potato cakes on kitchen paper and keep warm. Make two more potato cakes in the same way with the remaining mixture. Meanwhile, preheat the grill.

4 Cut the cheeses in half horizontally. Place one half cheese, cut-side up, on each potato cake *(right).* Grill for 2–3 minutes until golden. Garnish with thyme sprigs and serve at once with the salad.

SALADE MOUCLADE

Salade Mouclade aux Lentilles

Mouclade is a traditional recipe from La Rochelle in south-western France. The dish consists of mussels in a light, creamy curry sauce and is usually served hot. Here the flavours appear in a salad of warm lentils and lightly cooked spinach. Serve at room temperature during the summer months.

INGREDIENTS

45ml/3 tbsp olive oil, plus extra for drizzling
1 onion, finely chopped
350g/12oz/1¾ cups Puy or green lentils, soaked for 2 hours
900ml/1½ pints/3¾ cups vegetable stock
1.75kg/4–4½lb live mussels
75ml/5 tbsp dry white wine
2.5ml/½ tsp mild curry paste
pinch of saffron
30ml/2 tbsp double cream
2 large carrots, peeled
4 celery sticks
900g/2lb young spinach, stems removed
15ml/1 tbsp garlic oil
salt and cayenne pepper

SERVES 4

1 Heat the oil in a heavy saucepan and soften the onion for 6–8 minutes. Add the drained lentils and vegetable stock, bring to the boil and simmer for 45 minutes. Remove from the heat and and leave to cool.

2 Scrub the mussels well under cold running water. Remove the beards and discard any mussels that are open. Place in a large saucepan and add the wine. Cover and cook over a high heat, shaking the pan occasionally, for 5–8 minutes until the mussels have opened. Drain the mussels, reserving the liquid. Discard any not open. Allow to cool, then remove the shells.

3 Pass the mussel liquid through a fine sieve into a wide shallow saucepan, to remove any grit. Add the curry paste and saffron, then reduce over a high heat until almost dry. Remove from the heat, stir in the cream, season, and mix with the mussels.

4 Bring a saucepan of salted water to the boil. Cut the carrot and celery into 5cm/2in julienne strips, cook for 3 minutes, then remove from the pan, cool, and drizzle with olive oil.

5 Wash the spinach, put the wet leaves into a large saucepan, cover, and steam for 30 seconds. Drain the spinach under cold running water, then put the leaves into a colander and press dry with the back of a large spoon. Toss the spinach with the garlic oil, season with salt and cayenne pepper, and set aside.

6 Spoon the lentils into the centre of four large plates. Place five little piles of spinach around the edge of each one and put some carrot and celery strips on top of each pile. Spoon the mussels over the lentils and serve at room temperature.

GOLDEN CHEESE PUFFS

Aigrettes au Fromage

Serve these deep-fried puffs – known as *aigrettes* – with a fruity chutney and a green salad. Smaller, bite-size, ones make an excellent party snack.

INGREDIENTS

50g/2oz/½ cup plain flour
15g/½oz/1 tbsp butter
1 egg, plus 1 egg yolk, beaten
115g/4oz/1 cup finely grated mature Cheddar cheese
15ml/1 tbsp grated Parmesan cheese
2.5ml/½ tsp mustard powder
pinch of cayenne pepper
oil, for frying
salt and ground black pepper
mango chutney and salad, to serve

SERVES 4

1 Sift the flour on to a square of greaseproof paper and set aside. Place the butter and 150ml/¼ pint/⅔ cup water in a pan and heat until the butter is melted.

2 Bring the liquid to the boil and quickly tip in the flour all at once. Remove the pan from the heat and stir well with a wooden spoon until the mixture begins to leave the sides of the pan and forms a ball. Allow the mixture to cool slightly.

3 Gradually add the egg to the mixture, beating well after each addition. Stir in the cheeses, mustard, cayenne, and season.

4 Heat the oil in a large saucepan or deep-fat frier to 190°C/375°F or until a cube of bread browns in 30 seconds. Drop four spoonfuls of the cheese mixture at a time into the hot oil and deep-fry for 2–3 minutes until golden. Using a slotted spoon, lift out the cheese puffs and leave them to drain on kitchen paper. Keep them hot in the oven while cooking the remaining mixture. Allow two puffs per person and serve immediately with a generous spoonful of mango chutney and a green salad.

French Beans with Ham

Haricots Verts à la Poitrine Fumée

The subtle flavours of beans and unsmoked bacon combine well in this simple peasant dish. If you like, stir in some chopped fresh parsley just before serving.

INGREDIENTS

450g/1lb French beans
45ml/3 tbsp olive oil
1 onion, thinly sliced
2 garlic cloves, finely chopped
75g/3oz unsmoked bacon, rinded and chopped
salt and ground black pepper

SERVES 4

1 Cook the beans in boiling salted water for about 5–6 minutes, until just tender but still with a bit of bite.

2 Meanwhile, heat the oil in a pan, add the onion and fry for 5 minutes, until softened. Remove onion and set aside. Add the garlic and bacon and cook for 5 minutes. Return the onion to the pan (*right*).

3 Drain the beans, add to the pan and cook, stirring occasionally, for 2–3 minutes. Season well and serve hot.

Marinated Goat's Cheese with Herbs

Fromage de Chèvre aux Herbes et à l'Huile d'Olive

These little cheeses are delicious spread on toasted slices of French bread, brushed with olive oil and rubbed with garlic.

Ingredients

4 fresh soft goat's cheeses, halved
90ml/6 tbsp chopped fresh mixed parsley, thyme and oregano
2 garlic cloves, chopped
12 black peppercorns, lightly crushed
150ml/¼ pint/⅔ cup extra virgin olive oil
salad leaves, to serve

Serves 4–8

Cook's Tip

Any herbs can be added to the marinade – try chervil, tarragon, chives and basil. If you prefer, reserve the herb-flavoured oil, and use it to make a salad dressing.

1 Arrange the individual fresh goat's cheeses in a single layer in a large shallow non-metallic dish.

2 Put the chopped herbs, garlic and crushed peppercorns in a blender or food processor. Start the machine, then pour in the oil and process until the mixture is fairly smooth.

3 Spoon the herb mixture over the cheeses, then cover and leave to marinate in the fridge for 24 hours, basting the cheeses occasionally.

4 Remove the cheeses from the fridge about 30 minutes before serving and allow them to come to room temperature.

5 Serve the cheeses on a bed of salad leaves and spoon over a little of the olive oil and herb mixture.

Variation

For a subtle flavour and an attractive colour contrast, use pink peppercorns instead of black.

SALADE NIÇOISE

Salade Niçoise

alade Niçoise is the happy marriage of tuna fish, hard-boiled eggs, French beans and potatoes.

INGREDIENTS

675g/1½lb potatoes, peeled
225g/8oz French beans, trimmed
3 eggs, hard-boiled
1 cos lettuce
120ml/4fl oz/½ cup French dressing, see box below
225g/8oz small plum tomatoes, quartered
400g/14oz canned tuna in oil, drained
25g/1oz canned anchovy fillets
30ml/2 tbsp capers
12 black olives
salt and ground black pepper
basil leaves, to garnish (optional)

SERVES 4

COOK'S TIP

To make the French dressing, put 25ml/1½ tbsp white wine vinegar, 30ml/2 tbsp olive oil, 5ml/1 tsp Dijon mustard and 30ml/2 tbsp chopped, fresh mixed herbs in a screw-top jar, add salt and ground black pepper to taste and shake together.

1 Bring the potatoes to the boil in salted water and cook for 20 minutes. Boil the French beans for 6 minutes. Drain the potatoes and beans under cold running water and leave to cool.

2 Slice the potatoes thickly, and shell and quarter the eggs. Wash the lettuce and dry in a salad spinner or on a clean dish towel, then chop the leaves roughly. Put the lettuce into a large salad bowl and toss with half of the dressing.

3 Put the cooled potatoes, whole French beans and quartered tomatoes into a bowl and toss with the remaining French dressing, then arrange them decoratively over the bed of salad leaves in the salad bowl.

4 Break up the tuna fish into large flakes with a fork and distribute over the salad with the anchovy fillets, capers, and olives. Season to taste with salt and pepper and serve immediately. If you like, garnish with basil leaves.

GRILLED GARLIC MUSSELS

Moules Gratinées

The crunchy crumb topping provides a good contrast to the succulent mussels underneath in this flavoursome dish.

INGREDIENTS

1.5kg/3–3½lb live mussels
120ml/4fl oz/½ cup dry white wine
50g/2oz/4 tbsp butter
2 shallots, finely chopped
2 garlic cloves, crushed
50g/2oz/6 tbsp dried white breadcrumbs
60ml/4 tbsp chopped fresh mixed herbs, such as flat leaf parsley, basil and oregano
30ml/2 tbsp freshly grated Parmesan cheese
salt and ground black pepper
basil leaves, to garnish

SERVES 4

1 Scrub the mussels under cold running water. Remove the beards and discard any mussels that are open. Place in a pan with the wine. Cover and cook over a high heat, shaking the pan occasionally, for 5–8 minutes until the mussels have opened.

2 Strain the mussels and reserve the cooking liquid. Discard any that remain closed. Allow to cool slightly, then remove and discard the top half of each shell, leaving the mussels on the remaining halves.

3 Melt the butter in a large frying pan and fry the shallots until softened. Add the garlic and cook for 1–2 minutes.

4 Stir in the breadcrumbs and cook, stirring, until lightly browned. Remove from the heat and stir in the herbs. Moisten with a little of the reserved mussel liquid, then season to taste with salt and pepper. Preheat the grill.

5 Spoon the breadcrumb mixture over the mussels in their shells and arrange on baking sheets. Sprinkle with the grated Parmesan.

6 Cook the mussels under the hot grill in batches for about 2 minutes, until the topping is crisp and golden. Keep the cooked mussels warm in a low oven while grilling the remainder. Garnish with basil leaves and serve immediately.

FISH STEW

Soupe de Poisson

The broth of this dish is served as a starter, poured over bread, and the fish as the main course.

INGREDIENTS

225g/8oz/2 cups cooked unshelled prawns
450g/1lb mixed white fish fillets
45ml/3 tbsp olive oil
1 onion, chopped
1 leek, sliced
1 carrot, diced
1 garlic clove, chopped
2.5ml/½ tsp ground turmeric
150ml/¼ pint/⅔ cup dry white wine
400g/14oz can chopped tomatoes
fresh parsley, thyme and fennel sprigs
small piece of orange peel
1 cleaned squid, sliced
12 live mussels
salt and ground black pepper
Parmesan cheese shavings and chopped fresh parsley, to garnish

FOR THE ROUILLE SAUCE

2 slices white bread, crusts removed
2 garlic cloves, crushed
½ fresh red chilli
15ml/1 tbsp tomato purée
45–60ml/3–4 tbsp olive oil

SERVES 4

1 Peel the prawns leaving the tails on; cover and chill. Place all the prawn and fish trimmings in a pan and cover with 450ml/15fl oz/1⅞ cups water. Bring to the boil, then cover the pan and simmer for 30 minutes. Strain and reserve the stock.

2 Heat the oil in a large saucepan and add the onion, leek, carrot and garlic. Fry gently for 6–7 minutes, stir in the turmeric, wine, tomatoes and juice, fish stock, herbs and orange peel. Bring to the boil, cover, and simmer for about 20 minutes.

3 Meanwhile to make the rouille sauce, process the bread in a food processor or blender with the garlic, chilli and tomato purée. With the motor running, pour in the oil in a thin drizzle until the mixture is smooth and thickened.

4 Add the fish and seafood to the pan and simmer for 5–6 minutes, or until the fish is opaque and the mussels open. Remove the orange peel. Season. Serve in bowls with a spoonful of the rouille sauce and sprinkled with Parmesan and parsley.

Mediterranean Plaice Rolls

Roulades de Carrelets

Sun-dried tomatoes, pine nuts and anchovies make a flavoursome combination for the stuffing mixture for these plaice fillets.

Ingredients

4 plaice fillets, about 225g/8oz each, skinned
75g/3oz/6 tbsp butter
1 small onion, chopped
1 celery stick, finely chopped
115g/4oz/2 cups fresh white breadcrumbs
45ml/3 tbsp chopped fresh parsley
30ml/2 tbsp pine nuts, toasted
3–4 pieces sun-dried tomatoes in oil, drained and chopped
50g/2oz can anchovy fillets, drained and chopped
75ml/5 tbsp fish stock
ground black pepper

Serves 4

1 Preheat the oven to 180°C/350°F/Gas 4. Cut the plaice fillets in half lengthways to make eight smaller fillets.

2 Melt the butter in a pan and add the onion and celery. Cover and cook for 15 minutes, until soft. Do not brown.

3 Combine the breadcrumbs, parsley, pine nuts, sun-dried tomatoes and anchovies. Stir in the softened vegetables with the buttery juices and season with pepper.

4 Divide the stuffing into eight portions. Taking one portion at a time, form the stuffing into balls, then roll up each one inside a plaice fillet. Secure each roll with a cocktail stick.

5 Place the rolled-up fillets in a buttered ovenproof dish. Pour in the stock and cover the dish with a piece of buttered foil. Bake for about 20 minutes, or until the fish flakes easily when tested with a fork. Remove the cocktail sticks, then serve the plaice rolls with a little of the cooking juices drizzled over.

SOLE GOUJONS WITH LIME MAYONNAISE

Goujons de Sole Mayonnaise au Citron Vert

This simple dish can be rustled up very quickly. It makes an excellent light lunch or supper. If you cannot find a lime, use a small lemon instead.

INGREDIENTS

200ml/7fl oz/⅞ cup good-quality mayonnaise
1 small garlic clove, crushed
10ml/2 tsp capers, rinsed and chopped
10ml/2 tsp chopped gherkins
finely grated rind of ½ lime
10ml/2 tsp lime juice
15ml/1 tbsp chopped fresh coriander
675g/1½lb sole fillets, skinned
2 eggs, beaten
115g/4oz/2 cups fresh white breadcrumbs
oil, for deep-frying
salt and ground black pepper
lime wedges, to serve

SERVES 4

1 To make the lime mayonnaise, mix together the mayonnaise, garlic, capers, gherkins, lime rind and juice and chopped coriander. Season to taste with salt and pepper. Transfer to a serving bowl and chill until required.

2 Cut the sole fillets into finger-length strips. Dip into the beaten egg, then into the breadcrumbs.

3 Heat the oil in a deep-fat fryer to 180°C/350°F. Add the fish in batches and fry until golden brown and crisp. Drain on kitchen paper.

4 Pile the goujons on to warmed serving plates and serve them with the lime wedges for squeezing over. Hand round the sauce separately.

RED MULLET WITH FENNEL

Rougets au Fenouil

Whole mullet are excellent cooked in this way – you'll need only two fish if they are large. Fennel is a classic accompaniment to red mullet; the lemon butter sets off both flavours.

INGREDIENTS

3 small fennel bulbs
60ml/4 tbsp olive oil
2 small onions, thinly sliced
2–4 basil leaves
4 small or 2 large red mullet, cleaned
grated rind of ½ lemon
150ml/¼ pint/⅔ cup fish stock
50g/2oz/4 tbsp butter
juice of 1 lemon

SERVES 4

1 Snip off the feathery fronds from the fennel, chop finely and reserve for the garnish. Cut the fennel into wedges, leaving the layers attached at the root ends.

2 Heat the oil in a frying pan large enough to take the fish in a single layer. Add the fennel and onions and cook for 10–15 minutes, until softened and lightly browned.

3 Tuck a basil leaf inside each red mullet, then place the fish on top of the vegetables in the frying pan. Sprinkle the lemon rind over the fish. Pour in the stock and bring just to the boil. Cover the pan and cook gently for 15–20 minutes, until the fish are just tender.

4 Melt the butter in a small pan and, when it starts to sizzle and colour slightly, add the lemon juice. Pour the sauce over the fish, sprinkle with the reserved fennel fronds and serve immediately.

Tagliatelle with Saffron Mussels

Pâtes aux Moules Safranées

Mussels in a saffron and cream sauce are served with tagliatelle in this recipe, but you can use any other pasta if you prefer.

Ingredients

1.75kg/4–4½lb live mussels
150ml/¼ pint/⅔ cup dry white wine
2 shallots, chopped
350g/12oz dried tagliatelle
25g/1oz/2 tbsp butter
2 garlic cloves, crushed
250ml/8fl oz/1 cup double cream
generous pinch of saffron strands
1 egg yolk
salt and ground black pepper
30ml/2 tbsp chopped fresh parsley, to garnish

Serves 4

1 Scrub the mussels well under cold running water. Remove the beards and discard any mussels that are open. Place in a large pan with the wine and shallots. Cover and cook over a high heat, shaking the pan occasionally, for 5–8 minutes until the mussels have opened. Drain, reserving the liquid. Discard any not open. Shell all but a few of the mussels. Keep warm.

2 Cook the tagliatelle in a large pan of boiling salted water for about 10 minutes, until *al dente.*

3 Meanwhile bring the reserved cooking liquid to the boil, then reduce by half. Strain into a jug to remove any grit. Melt the butter in another saucepan and fry the garlic for 1 minute.

4 Add the mussel liquid, cream and saffron and heat gently until the sauce thickens slightly. Off the heat, stir in the egg yolk, shelled mussels and seasoning.

5 Drain the tagliatelle and transfer to warmed plates. Spoon the sauce over, garnish with chopped parsley and reserved mussels and serve at once.

CHILLI PRAWNS

Grosses Crevettes à la Tomate Epicée

This spicy combination of large prawns with tomatoes and a chopped red chilli makes a lovely light main course for a casual supper. Serve with rice, noodles or freshly cooked pasta and a leafy salad.

INGREDIENTS

45ml/3 tbsp olive oil
2 shallots, chopped
2 garlic cloves, chopped
1 fresh red chilli, chopped
450g/1lb ripe tomatoes, peeled, seeded and chopped
15ml/1 tbsp tomato purée
1 bay leaf
1 thyme sprig
90ml/6 tbsp dry white wine
450g/1lb cooked, peeled large prawns
salt and ground black pepper
roughly torn basil leaves, to garnish

SERVES 3–4

COOK'S TIP

For a milder flavour, remove all the seeds from the chilli.

1 Heat the oil in a pan, then add the shallots, garlic and chilli and fry until the garlic starts to brown.

2 Add the tomatoes, tomato purée, bay leaf, thyme, wine and seasoning. Bring to the boil, then reduce the heat and cook gently for about 10 minutes, stirring occasionally, until the sauce has thickened. Discard the herbs.

3 Stir the prawns into the sauce and heat through for a few minutes. Taste and adjust the seasoning. Scatter over the basil leaves and serve at once.

SALMON WITH WATERCRESS SAUCE

Saumon au Cresson

Adding the watercress to the sauce right at the end of cooking retains much of its flavour and colour. A lovely dish for summer.

INGREDIENTS

300ml/½ pint/1¼ cups double cream
30ml/2 tbsp chopped fresh tarragon
25g/1oz/2 tbsp unsalted butter
15ml/1 tbsp sunflower oil
4 salmon fillets, about 175g/6oz each, skinned and boned
1 garlic clove, crushed
120ml/4fl oz/½ cup dry white wine
1 bunch watercress
salt and ground black pepper
lettuce, to serve

SERVES 4

1 Gently heat the cream in a small pan until just beginning to boil. Remove from the heat and stir in half the tarragon. Leave to infuse while cooking the fish.

2 Heat the butter and oil in a pan, add the salmon and fry for 3–5 minutes on each side. Remove and keep warm. Add the garlic and fry for 1 minute, then add the wine and boil until reduced to about 15ml/1 tbsp.

3 Meanwhile, strip the leaves off the watercress stalks and chop finely.

4 Strain the cream into the pan and gently cook for just a few minutes, stirring until thickened. Stir in the remaining tarragon and the watercress, then cook for a few minutes, until wilted but still bright green *(right)*. Season and serve at once, spooned over the salmon. Serve with lettuce.

GRILLED SARDINES

Sardines Grillées

The full flavour of fresh sardines needs very little to enhance it. Here it is simply complemented by lemon and parsley.

INGREDIENTS

75ml/5 tbsp olive oil
juice of 1 lemon
5ml/1 tsp finely grated lemon rind
30ml/2 tbsp chopped fresh parsley
8–12 fresh sardines (depending on size)
salt and ground black pepper
tomato and spring onion salad and hot garlic bread, to serve

SERVES 4

1 Preheat the grill. In a small bowl, mix together the oil, lemon juice and rind, parsley and seasoning.

2 Scale the sardines under running water by rubbing the skin with your fingers from the tail towards the head. Slit the belly and remove the innards, rinse, and pat dry. Make two slashes in the skin on both sides of each sardine *(left)*.

3 Brush the sardines all over with the prepared marinade and arrange them on the grill rack.

4 Cook under a moderate heat for about 2–3 minutes, basting once, until the skin is starting to crispen, and then carefully turn the fish over. Brush with some more of the marinade. Grill for a further 2–3 minutes.

5 Lift the sardines carefully on to a warmed serving platter and pour over the remaining marinade. Serve with tomato and spring onion salad and hot garlic bread.

Trout with Mushroom Sauce

Truites aux Champignons

A simple sauce made with wild or cultivated mushrooms, white wine and cream perfectly complements the flavour of trout. This recipe is a favourite all over rural France.

Ingredients

8 trout fillets
seasoned plain flour, for dusting
75g/3oz/6 tbsp butter
1 garlic clove, chopped
10ml/2 tsp chopped fresh sage
350g/12oz mixed wild or cultivated mushrooms, sliced
90ml/6 tbsp dry white wine
250ml/8fl oz/1 cup double cream
salt and ground black pepper
fresh sage sprigs, to garnish

Serves 4

Cook's Tip

Use a large sharp knife to ease the skin from the trout fillets, then pull out any bones from the flesh – a pair of tweezers makes easy work of this fiddly task!

1 Remove the skin from the trout fillets, then carefully remove any bones. Lightly dust the fillets on both sides with the seasoned flour, shaking off any excess.

2 Melt the butter in a large frying pan, add the trout fillets and fry gently over a moderate heat for 4–5 minutes, turning once. Remove from the pan and keep warm.

3 Add the garlic, sage and mushrooms to the pan and fry until softened. Pour in the wine and boil briskly to allow the alcohol to evaporate. Stir in the cream and season with salt and pepper.

4 Serve the trout fillets on warmed plates with the sauce spooned over. Garnish with fresh sage sprigs.

Variation

Omit the sage and substitute 15ml/1 tbsp pastis for the 90ml/6 tbsp dry white wine.

Coq au Vin

Coq au Vin

Chicken joints flamed in brandy then cooked in red wine create the base of this delicious, rich casserole. Serve with potatoes and a green vegetable.

INGREDIENTS

60ml/4 tbsp flour
1.5kg/3–3½lb chicken, cut into 8 pieces
15ml/1 tbsp olive oil
50g/2oz/4 tbsp butter
20 button onions
75g/3oz piece of bacon without rind, diced
about 20 button mushrooms
30ml/2 tbsp brandy
1 bottle red Burgundy
bouquet garni
3 garlic cloves
5ml/1 tsp soft light brown sugar
15g/½oz/1 tbsp butter, softened
salt and ground black pepper
flat leaf parsley, chopped fresh parsley and croûtons, to garnish

SERVES 4

1 Place 45ml/3 tbsp of the flour and the seasoning in a large plastic bag and shake each chicken piece in it until lightly coated.

2 Heat the oil and butter in a large flameproof casserole. Add the onions and bacon and sauté for 3–4 minutes, until the onions are lightly browned. Add the button mushrooms and fry for 2 minutes. Remove all the vegetables with a slotted spoon, and set aside.

3 Add the chicken pieces to the hot oil and cook for about 5–6 minutes until browned on all sides.

4 Pour in the brandy and (standing well back from the pan) carefully light it with a match, then shake the pan gently until the flames subside. When the flames have died down, pour in the wine, then add the bouquet garni, garlic, sugar and seasoning.

5 Bring to the boil, cover, and simmer for 1 hour, stirring occasionally. Return the reserved onions, bacon and mushrooms to the casserole, cover, and cook for 30 minutes. Transfer the chicken, vegetables and bacon to a warmed dish.

6 Remove the bouquet garni and boil rapidly for 2 minutes to reduce slightly. Cream the butter and remaining flour and whisk in teaspoonfuls of the mixture until the liquid has thickened slightly. Pour over the chicken, garnish with parsley and serve with croûtons.

POUSSINS WITH GRAPES IN VERMOUTH

Poussins aux Raisins et au Vermouth

The aromatic herbs used to flavour vermouth, combined with sweet white grapes, make a beautiful sauce to accompany these little birds.

INGREDIENTS

4 oven-ready poussins, about 450g/1lb each
50g/2oz/4 tbsp butter, softened
2 shallots, chopped
60ml/4 tbsp chopped fresh parsley
225g/8oz white grapes, preferably muscatel, halved and seeded
150ml/¼ pint/⅔ cup dry white vermouth
5ml/1 tsp cornflour
60ml/4 tbsp double cream
salt and ground black pepper
30ml/2 tbsp pine nuts, toasted
watercress sprigs, to garnish

SERVES 4

1 Preheat the oven to 200°C/400°F/Gas 6. Wash and dry the poussins. Spread the softened butter all over the birds and put a hazelnut-size piece in the cavity of each bird. Mix together the shallots and parsley.

2 Place a quarter of the shallot mixture inside each bird. Put them in a roasting tin and roast for 40–50 minutes, or until the juices run clear when the thickest part of the flesh is pierced with a skewer. Transfer to a warmed platter and keep warm.

3 Skim off most of the fat from the tin, then add the grapes and vermouth. Place the tin over a low heat for a few minutes to warm the grapes.

4 Lift the grapes out of the tin with a slotted spoon and scatter them around the birds. Keep covered. Stir the cornflour into the cream, then add to the pan juices. Cook gently for a few minutes, stirring, until the sauce has thickened. Taste and adjust the seasoning.

5 Pour the sauce around the poussins. Sprinkle with the toasted pine nuts and garnish with watercress sprigs.

NORMANDY PHEASANT

Faisan à la Normande

Normandy is famed for its dairy farms and apple orchards. This recipe, with its apples, cider, Calvados, butter and cream, makes the most of its produce.

INGREDIENTS

2 oven-ready pheasants
15ml/1 tbsp olive oil
25g/1oz/2 tbsp butter
60ml/4 tbsp Calvados
450ml/¾ pint/1⅞ cups dry cider
bouquet garni
3 eating apples, peeled, cored and thickly sliced
150ml/¼ pint/⅔ cup double cream
salt and ground black pepper
thyme sprigs, to garnish

SERVES 4

1 Preheat the oven to 160°C/325°F/Gas 3. Joint both pheasants into four pieces. Discard the backbones and knuckles.

2 Heat the oil and butter in a large flameproof casserole. Working in two batches, add the pheasant pieces to the casserole and brown them over a high heat. Once browned return all the pheasant pieces to the casserole.

3 Standing well back, pour the Calvados over the pheasant pieces and set it alight. When the flames have subsided, pour in the cider, then add the bouquet garni and seasoning and bring to the boil. Cover and cook for 50 minutes.

4 Tuck the apple slices around the pheasant. Cover and cook for 5–10 minutes, or until the pheasant is tender. Transfer the pheasant and apple slices to a warmed serving plate, cover and keep warm. Remove the bouquet garni.

5 Reduce the sauce by half, stir in the cream and simmer for 2–3 minutes until thickened. Spoon over the pheasant and serve at once, garnished with thyme sprigs.

Breton Pork and Bean Casserole

Porc aux Haricots

There are many versions of this classic dish, developed in the different regions of France. Some include goose and duck as well.

Ingredients

30ml/2 tbsp olive oil
1 onion, chopped
2 garlic cloves, chopped
450g/1lb lean shoulder of pork, cubed
350g/12oz lean lamb (preferably leg), trimmed and cubed
225g/8oz coarse pork and garlic sausage, cut into chunks
400g/14oz can chopped tomatoes
30ml/2 tbsp red wine
15ml/1 tbsp tomato purée
bouquet garni
400g/14oz can cannellini beans, drained
50g/2oz/1 cup wholemeal breadcrumbs
salt and ground black pepper
salad and French bread, to serve

Serves 4

Cook's Tip

Replace the lamb with duck breast, if you like, but be sure to drain off any fat before sprinkling with the breadcrumbs.

1 Preheat the oven to 160°C/325°F/Gas 3. Heat the oil in a large flameproof casserole and fry the onion and garlic over a low heat until softened. Remove with a slotted spoon and reserve.

2 Add the pork, lamb and sausage cubes to the casserole, in batches if necessary, and fry over a high heat for a few minutes, stirring occasionally, until they are browned on all sides. Return the onion and garlic to the casserole and stir them into the meat.

3 Stir in the tomatoes, wine and tomato purée and add 300ml/½ pint/1¼ cups water. Season well and add the bouquet garni. Cover and bring to the boil, then transfer to the oven and cook for 1½ hours.

4 Remove the bouquet garni, stir in the beans and sprinkle the breadcrumbs over the top. Return the casserole to the oven, uncovered, for 30 minutes, until the top is golden brown. Serve hot with a green salad and French bread to mop up the juices.

RICH BEEF CASSEROLE

Boeuf au Vin Rouge

This full-bodied dish should be served with mashed potatoes to absorb its delicious sauce. It is a perfect meal for a winter's day.

INGREDIENTS

1kg/2¼lb chuck steak, cut into cubes
2 onions, coarsely chopped
bouquet garni
6 black peppercorns
15ml/1 tbsp red wine vinegar
1 bottle full-bodied red wine
45–60ml/3–4 tbsp olive oil
3 celery sticks, thickly sliced
50g/2oz/½ cup plain flour
300ml/½ pint/1¼ cups beef stock
30ml/2 tbsp tomato purée
2 garlic cloves, crushed
175g/6oz chestnut mushrooms, halved
400g/14oz can artichoke hearts, drained and halved
chopped fresh parsley and thyme, to garnish
creamy mashed potatoes, to serve

SERVES 4

1 Place the meat cubes in a large bowl. Add the onions, bouquet garni, peppercorns, vinegar and red wine. Stir well, cover and leave to marinate overnight.

2 The next day, preheat the oven to 160°C/325°F/Gas 3. Using a slotted spoon, remove the meat cubes and onions from the marinade, reserving the marinade. Pat the meat and onions dry.

3 Heat the oil in a large flameproof casserole and fry the meat and onions in batches, adding a little more oil, if necessary. Remove and set aside.

4 Add the celery to the casserole and fry until lightly browned. Remove and set aside with the meat and onions.

5 Sprinkle the flour into the casserole and cook for 1 minute. Gradually add the reserved marinade and the stock, and bring to the boil, stirring. Return the meat, onions and celery to the casserole, then stir in the tomato purée and crushed garlic.

6 Cover the casserole and cook in the oven for about 2¼ hours. Stir in the chestnut mushrooms and artichokes, cover again and return to the oven for a further 15 minutes, until the meat is tender. Garnish with chopped parsley and thyme, and serve hot with creamy mashed potatoes.

POT-ROAST POUSSINS

Poussins au Céleri

This method of cooking keeps the poussins moist and succulent, and provides a whole meal cooked in one dish. Serve it in spring or early summer.

INGREDIENTS

15ml/1 tbsp olive oil
1 onion, sliced
1 large garlic clove, sliced
50g/2oz/½ cup diced lightly smoked bacon
2 fresh poussins, just under 450g/1lb each
30ml/2 tbsp butter, melted
2 baby celery hearts, each cut into 4
8 baby carrots
2 small courgettes, cut into chunks
8 small new potatoes
600ml/1 pint/2½ cups chicken stock
150ml/¼ pint/⅔ cup dry white wine
1 bay leaf
2 fresh thyme sprigs
2 fresh rosemary sprigs
15ml/1 tbsp butter, softened
15ml/1 tbsp plain flour
salt and ground black pepper
fresh herbs, to garnish

SERVES 2–4

1 Preheat the oven to 190°C/375°F/Gas 5. Heat the olive oil in a large flameproof casserole, add the onion, garlic and bacon and sauté for 5–6 minutes.

2 Brush the poussins with a little of the melted butter and season well. Lay them on top of the onion mixture and arrange the prepared vegetables around them. Pour the chicken stock and wine around the birds and add the herbs. Cover, bake for 20 minutes, then remove the lid and brush the birds with the remaining melted butter. Bake for a further 25–30 minutes until golden.

3 Transfer the poussins to warmed serving plates. Remove the vegetables with a slotted spoon and arrange them round the birds. Cover with foil and keep warm.

4 Discard the herbs from the pan juices. In a bowl, mix together the butter and flour to form a thick paste. Bring the liquid in the pan to the boil and then whisk in a few teaspoonfuls of the paste, until thickened. Taste the sauce for seasoning and add salt and pepper if necessary. Serve the poussins, cut in half if wished, with the vegetables. Garnish with fresh herb sprigs.

RATATOUILLE

Ratatouille

A wonderful casserole of vegetables that can be served as a starter, main course or side-dish, and is equally good both hot or cold.

INGREDIENTS

2 large aubergines, coarsely chopped
4 courgettes, coarsely chopped
150ml/¼ pint/⅔ cup olive oil
2 onions, sliced
2 garlic cloves, chopped
1 large red pepper, seeded and coarsely chopped
2 large yellow peppers, seeded and coarsely chopped
fresh rosemary sprig
fresh thyme sprig
5ml/1 tsp coriander seeds, crushed
3 plum tomatoes, skinned, seeded and chopped
8 basil leaves, torn
salt and ground black pepper
fresh parsley or basil sprigs, to garnish

SERVES 4

1 Sprinkle the aubergines and courgettes with salt, and then place them in a colander with a plate and a weight on top to extract the bitter juices. Leave them to stand for about 30 minutes.

2 Heat the olive oil in a large pan. Add the onions, fry gently for about 6–7 minutes, until just softened, then add the garlic and cook for another 2 minutes.

COOK'S TIP

For extra flavour, stir in a handful of stoned halved black or green olives immediately before serving.

3 Rinse the aubergines and courgettes and pat dry with kitchen paper. Add to the pan with the peppers, increase the heat and sauté until the peppers are just turning brown. Add the herbs and coriander seeds, then cover the pan and cook gently for about 40 minutes.

4 Add the tomatoes and season well. Cook gently for 10 minutes, until the vegetables are soft but not too mushy. Remove the herb sprigs. Stir in the basil leaves and taste for seasoning. Serve warm or cold, garnished with sprigs of parsley or basil.

Onion Tart

Tarte à l'Oignon

The Provençal version of pizza, this is a versatile dish that can be served hot or cold. It is ideal for summer picnics.

Ingredients

275g/10oz packet pizza base mix
5ml/1 tsp olive oil, plus extra for drizzling

For the Topping

30ml/2 tbsp olive oil
6 onions, thinly sliced
2 garlic cloves, crushed
50g/2oz can anchovy fillets, sliced in half lengthways
8 black olives, stoned
10ml/2 tsp chopped fresh thyme, or 2.5ml/½ tsp dried thyme
salt and ground black pepper

Serves 6

1 Heat the oil in a frying pan, add the sliced onions and garlic and season lightly. Fry gently, stirring occasionally, for about 40 minutes, or until the onions are soft but not too brown.

2 Preheat the oven to 220°C/425°F/Gas 7. Empty the pizza base mix into a bowl, stir in 250ml/8fl oz/1 cup warm water and add the oil. Mix to a dough and then knead for about 5 minutes.

3 Lightly grease a 33 × 23cm/13 × 9in Swiss roll tin. Roll out the dough on a lightly floured surface to fit the tin and press into the base. Spread the cooked onions evenly over the dough and then arrange the anchovy fillets on top in a lattice pattern. Scatter over the olives and chopped thyme and drizzle with a little olive oil. Place in a large sealed plastic bag and leave to rise in a warm place for 15 minutes.

4 Bake for 10 minutes. Reduce the oven temperature to 190°C/375°F/Gas 5 and cook for 15–20 minutes or until golden brown around the edges. Serve warm or cold.

PROVENÇAL BEANS

Haricots à la Provençale

Much of the cuisine of Provence is based on the tomato. Here tomatoes and garlic transform plain beans into a memorable dish.

INGREDIENTS

5ml/1 tsp olive oil
1 small onion, finely chopped
1 garlic clove, crushed
225g/8oz runner beans, trimmed and sliced
225g/8oz French beans, trimmed and sliced
2 tomatoes, peeled and chopped
salt and ground black pepper

SERVES 4

1 Heat the oil in a heavy-based saucepan and sauté the onion over a medium heat until softened but not browned.

2 Add the garlic and sauté for 1–2 minutes, then stir in the sliced runner beans, French beans and chopped tomatoes. Season generously with salt and pepper, (left), then cover the pan tightly with a lid.

3 Cook over a fairly low heat, shaking the pan occasionally, for about 30 minutes, or until the beans are tender. Serve hot.

Mushroom Medley

Fricassée de Champignons

The wonderful range of mushrooms – both fresh and dried – available in France is put to good use in this exciting side dish.

Ingredients

15g/½oz packet dried ceps or porcini mushrooms (optional)
60ml/4 tbsp olive oil
225g/8oz button mushrooms, halved or sliced
115g/4oz oyster mushrooms
115g/4oz fresh shiitake mushrooms, or 25g/1oz dried and soaked mushrooms
2 garlic cloves, crushed
10ml/2 tsp ground coriander
45ml/3 tbsp chopped fresh parsley
salt and ground black pepper

Serves 4

1 If you are using dried ceps or porcini mushrooms (and they do give a good rich flavour), soak them in a little hot water just to cover for 20 minutes.

2 In a large saucepan, heat the oil and add all the mushrooms, including the soaked ceps or porcini, if using. Stir well, cover and cook gently for 5 minutes.

3 Crush the garlic and add to the pan with the coriander and seasoning. Stir well then cook for a further 5 minutes, until the mushrooms are tender and much of the liquid has been reduced. Stir in the chopped parsley, then allow the mushrooms to cool slightly before serving.

POTATO GRATIN

Gratin de Pommes de Terre

This tasty potato dish is perfect for a light supper or lunch dish. For a more substantial meal, serve with roast chicken or lamb chops and add a green vegetable or salad.

INGREDIENTS

1 garlic clove
5 large baking potatoes, peeled
45ml/3 tbsp freshly grated Parmesan cheese
600ml/1 pint/2½ cups vegetable or chicken stock
pinch of freshly grated nutmeg
salt and ground black pepper

SERVES 4

1 Preheat the oven to 200°C/400°F/Gas 6. Halve the garlic clove and rub over the base and sides of a gratin dish measuring about 20 × 30cm/8 × 12in.

2 Slice the potatoes very thinly and arrange a third of them in the dish Sprinkle with a little grated cheese, salt and pepper. Pour over some of the stock.

3 Continue layering the potatoes and cheese as before, then pour over the rest of the stock. Sprinkle with nutmeg.

4 Bake in the oven for 1¼–1½ hours or until the potatoes are tender and the tops well browned.

COOK'S TIP

For a potato and onion gratin, slice an onion and layer with the potato.

Chicory, Carrot and Rocket Salad

Salade Mélangée d'Endives, Carottes et Roquette

A bright and colourful salad which is ideal for a buffet or barbecue party. If you cannot find rocket, baby spinach or watercress can be used instead.

Ingredients

3 carrots, coarsely grated
about 50g/2oz fresh rocket, roughly chopped
1 large head of chicory, separated into leaves

For the Dressing

45ml/3 tbsp sunflower oil
15ml/1 tbsp hazelnut or walnut oil (optional)
30ml/2 tbsp cider or white wine vinegar
10ml/2 tsp clear honey
5ml/1 tsp grated lemon rind
15ml/1 tbsp poppy seeds
salt and ground black pepper

Serves 4–6

1 Mix together the carrots and rocket in a large bowl and season well.

2 Shake the dressing ingredients together in a screw-top jar then pour on to the carrot mixture. Toss the salad thoroughly.

3 Line shallow salad bowls with the chicory leaves and spoon the salad into the centre *(right)*. Serve lightly chilled.

CHOCOLATE CHESTNUT ROULADE

Roulade au Chocolat et aux Marrons

This moist chocolate sponge has a soft, mousse-like texture as it contains no flour. Don't worry if it cracks as you roll it up – this is typical of a good roulade.

INGREDIENTS

175g/6oz plain chocolate
30ml/2 tbsp strong black coffee
5 eggs, separated
175g/6oz/¾ cup caster sugar
250ml/8fl oz/1 cup double cream
225g/8oz unsweetened chestnut purée
45–60ml/3–4 tbsp icing sugar, plus extra for dusting
single cream, to serve

SERVES 8

1 Preheat the oven to 180°C/350°F/Gas 4. Line a 33 × 23cm/13 × 9in Swiss roll tin with non-stick greaseproof paper and brush lightly with oil.

2 Break the chocolate into a bowl and set over a saucepan of barely simmering water. Allow the chocolate to melt, then stir until smooth. Remove the bowl from the pan and stir in the coffee. Leave to cool slightly.

3 Whisk together the egg yolks and caster sugar in a separate bowl, until they are thick and light, then stir in the cooled chocolate mixture.

4 Whisk the egg whites in another bowl until they hold stiff peaks. Stir a spoonful into the chocolate mixture to lighten it, then gently fold in the rest.

5 Pour the mixture into the prepared tin, and gently spread with a rubber spatula to level the surface. Bake for 20 minutes. Remove the roulade from the oven, then cover with a clean dish towel and leave to cool in the tin for several hours, or overnight.

6 Put the double cream into a large bowl and whip until it forms soft peaks. In another bowl, mix together the chestnut purée and icing sugar until smooth, then fold into the whipped cream.

7 Lay a piece of greaseproof paper on the work surface and dust with icing sugar. Turn out the roulade on to the paper and carefully peel off the lining paper. Trim the sides. Gently spread the chestnut cream evenly over the roulade to within 2.5cm/1in of the edges.

8 Using the greaseproof paper to help you, carefully roll up the roulade as tightly and evenly as possible.

9 Chill the roulade for 2 hours, then sprinkle liberally with icing sugar. Serve in thick slices with a little single cream.

COOK'S TIP

Make sure that you whisk the egg yolks and sugar for at least 5 minutes to incorporate as much air as possible.

CHOCOLATE PROFITEROLES

Profiteroles au Chocolat

These luscious pastries are a favourite dessert in France. For perfect choux pastry, it is important that the flour is added quickly and all at once to the boiling liquid.

INGREDIENTS

65g/2½oz/⅔ cup plain flour
pinch of salt
50g/2oz/4 tbsp butter
2 eggs, beaten
450ml/15fl oz/1⅞ cups whipping cream
115g/4oz plain chocolate

MAKES 24

1 Preheat the oven to 220°C/425°F/Gas 7. Grease two baking sheets. Sift the flour and salt on to a sheet of paper. Put the butter and 150ml/¼ pint/⅔ cup water into a pan and heat gently until the butter has melted. Bring to the boil and then tip in the flour all at once. Remove from the heat. Beat until the mixture forms a ball and leaves the sides of the pan. Cool slightly.

2 Gradually add the beaten eggs, beating well after each addition, until a smooth, thick paste is formed. Spoon into a large piping bag with a 1cm/½in plain nozzle.

3 Pipe 24 walnut-size balls on to the baking sheets. Bake at the top of the oven for 20–25 minutes. Make a slit in each one for the steam to escape, then return to the oven for 5 minutes. Cool on a wire rack.

4 Place all but 60ml/4 tbsp of the cream in a bowl, whip until just thick, then spoon into a large piping bag fitted with a plain nozzle. Cut each profiterole in half, fill with cream and reassemble.

5 To make the chocolate sauce, place the chocolate in a pan with 60ml/4 tbsp water and the reserved 60ml/4 tbsp cream. Heat gently over a very low heat until the chocolate has melted. Pile all the profiteroles in a pyramid on a serving dish and pour the hot sauce over them just before serving.

TARTE TATIN

Tarte Tatin

This delicious caramelized fruit tart was created by the Tatin sisters who ran a restaurant in Sologne in the Orléanais around the turn of the century.

INGREDIENTS

FOR THE PASTRY

50g/2oz/4 tbsp butter, softened

40g/1½ oz/3 tbsp caster sugar

1 egg

115g/4oz/1 cup plain flour

pinch of salt

FOR THE APPLE LAYER

75g/3oz/6 tbsp butter, softened

115g/4oz/generous ½ cup soft light brown sugar

10 firm eating apples, peeled, cored and thickly sliced

whipped cream, to serve

SERVES 4

1 To make the pastry, cream the butter and sugar in a bowl until pale and creamy. Beat in the egg, then sift in the flour and salt and mix to a soft dough. Knead the dough lightly on a floured surface, then wrap in clear film and chill for 1 hour.

2 Grease a 23cm/9in cake tin, then add 50g/2oz/4 tbsp of the butter. Place the cake tin on the burner and melt the butter gently. Remove and sprinkle with 65g/2½ oz/⅓ cup of the sugar.

3 Arrange the apple slices on top, then sprinkle with the remaining sugar and dot with the remaining butter.

4 Preheat the oven to 230°C/450°F/Gas 8. Place the cake tin on the burner again, over a low to medium heat, for about 15 minutes, until a light golden caramel forms on the bottom. Remove from the heat.

5 Roll out the pastry on a lightly floured surface to a round the same size as the tin and lay on top of the apples. Tuck the pastry edges round the sides of the apples.

6 Bake the tart for about 20–25 minutes, until the pastry is golden. Remove the tart from the oven and leave it to stand for about 5 minutes.

7 Place an upturned plate on top of the cake tin and, holding the two together with a dish towel, turn the apple tart out on to the plate. Serve the tart while still warm with whipped cream.

CREPES SUZETTE

Crêpes Suzette

An impressive dessert, ideal for serving at the end of a formal dinner party. For a special touch, flame the brandy as you pour it into the pan.

INGREDIENTS

115g/4oz/1 cup plain flour
pinch of salt
1 egg
1 egg yolk
300ml/½ pint/1¼ cups skimmed milk
15ml/1 tbsp unsalted butter, melted, plus extra for frying

FOR THE SAUCE

2 large oranges
50g/2oz/4 tbsp butter
115g/4oz/generous ½ cup soft light brown sugar
15ml/1 tbsp Grand Marnier
15ml/1 tbsp brandy

MAKES 8

1 Sift the flour and salt into a bowl and make a well in the centre. Add the egg and the extra yolk into the well. Stir with a wooden spoon to incorporate the flour from around the edges.

2 When the mixture thickens, gradually pour on the milk, beating well after each addition, until a smooth batter is formed. Stir in the butter, transfer to a measuring jug, cover and chill.

3 Heat a 20cm/8in shallow frying pan, add a little butter and heat until sizzling. Pour in a little of the batter, tilting the pan back and forth to cover the base thinly.

4 Cook the crêpes over a medium heat for 1–2 minutes until lightly browned underneath, then flip over with a spatula and cook for 1 minute. Repeat this process until you have eight crêpes. Pile them up on a plate as they are ready.

5 Pare the rind from one of the oranges and reserve 5ml/1 tsp for decoration. Squeeze the juice from both oranges.

6 To make the sauce, melt the butter in a large frying pan and add the sugar, orange rind and juice. Heat gently until the sugar has dissolved and the mixture is bubbling. Fold each crêpe in quarters. Add to the pan one at a time, coat in the sauce and fold in half again. Push to the side of the pan to make room for the others.

7 Pour on the Grand Marnier and brandy and cook gently for 2–3 minutes, until the sauce has slightly caramelized. Serve, sprinkled with the reserved orange rind.

Pear and Hazelnut Flan

Tarte aux Poires

A delicious flan for a special meal. If you prefer use ground almonds instead of the hazelnuts. If the filling mixture is a little thick, stir in some of the pear juice.

Ingredients

115g/4oz/1 cup plain flour
115g/4oz/¾ cup wholemeal flour
115g/4oz/8 tbsp sunflower margarine
45ml/3 tbsp cold water

For the Filling

50g/2oz/½ cup self-raising flour
115g/4oz/1 cup ground hazelnuts
5ml/1 tsp vanilla essence
50g/2oz caster sugar
50g/2oz/4 tbsp butter, softened
2 eggs, beaten
45ml/3 tbsp raspberry jam
400g/14oz can pears in natural juice
a few chopped hazelnuts, to decorate

Serves 6–8

1 Stir the flours together in a large mixing bowl, then rub in the margarine until the mixture resembles fine crumbs. Mix to a firm dough with the water.

2 Roll out the pastry and use it to line a 23–25cm/9–10in flan tin, pressing it firmly up the sides after trimming, so the pastry sits above the tin a little. Prick the base, line with greaseproof paper and fill with baking beans. Chill for 30 minutes.

3 Preheat the oven to 200°C/400°F/Gas 6. Place the flan tin on a baking sheet and bake for 20 minutes, removing the paper and beans for the last 5 minutes.

4 Meanwhile to make the filling, beat together all the ingredients except for the jam and pears.

5 Reduce the oven temperature to 180°C/350°F/Gas 4. Spread the jam on the pastry case base and spoon over the filling. Drain the pears well and arrange them, cut-side down, in the filling. Scatter with the nuts and bake for 30 minutes until golden brown and set.

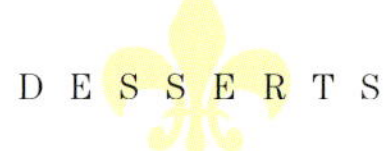

APRICOT AND ALMOND JALOUSIE

Jalousie aux Amandes et à l'Abricot

Jalousie means "shutter" in French, and the traditional slatted puff pastry topping of this fruit pie looks exactly like the shutters outside the windows of French houses.

INGREDIENTS

225g/8oz ready-made puff pastry
a little beaten egg
90ml/6 tbsp apricot preserve
30ml/2 tbsp caster sugar
30ml/2 tbsp flaked almonds
cream or natural yogurt, to serve

SERVES 4

1 Preheat the oven to 220°C/425°F/Gas 7. Roll out the pastry on a lightly floured surface and cut into a 30cm/12in square. Cut in half to make two rectangles.

2 Place one piece of pastry on a wetted baking sheet and brush all round the edges with beaten egg. Spread over the apricot preserve.

3 Fold the remaining rectangle in half lengthways and cut about eight diagonal slits from the centre fold to within about 1cm/½in of the edge all the way along.

4 Unfold the pastry and place it on top of the preserve-covered pastry on the baking sheet, matching each edge carefully to the base. Press the pastry edges together well to seal and scallop the edges at close intervals with the back of a small knife.

5 Brush the slashed pastry top with a little water and sprinkle evenly with the sugar and the flaked almonds.

6 Bake in the oven for 25–30 minutes, until well risen and golden brown. Remove the jalousie from the oven and leave to cool on a wire rack. Serve the jalousie sliced, with cream or natural yogurt.

CREME CARAMEL

Crème Caramel

This creamy, caramel-flavoured custard now enjoys worldwide popularity. Do not put too much water into the roasting tin or it may bubble over into the ramekins.

INGREDIENTS

90g/3½ oz/½ cup granulated sugar
300ml/½ pint/1¼ cups milk
300ml/½ pint/1¼ cups single cream
6 eggs
90ml/6 tbsp caster sugar
2.5ml/½ tsp vanilla essence

SERVES 6

1 Preheat the oven to 150°C/300°F/Gas 2 and half fill a large, deep roasting tin with water. Set aside until needed.

2 To make the caramel topping, place the granulated sugar in a small saucepan with 60ml/4 tbsp water and heat it gently, swirling the pan from time to time, until dissolved. Increase the heat and boil, without stirring, to a good caramel colour.

3 Immediately pour the caramel into six ramekin dishes. Place the dishes in the roasting tin and set aside.

4 To make the egg custard, heat the milk and cream together in a pan until almost boiling. Meanwhile, beat together the eggs, caster sugar and vanilla essence.

5 Whisk the hot milk into the eggs and sugar, then pour the liquid through a sieve on to the cooled caramel bases.

6 Bake in the oven for 1½–2 hours (topping up the water level after about 1 hour), or until the custards have set in the centre. Lift out the dishes and leave to cool, then cover and chill overnight.

7 Loosen the sides of the chilled custards with a knife and invert on to serving plates, allowing the caramel sauce to run down the sides.

INDEX